Maths Made Easy

COLOUR A SPACESHIP OR PLANET WHEN YOU COMPLETE A PAGE.

Compiled by John Drinkwater
Illustrated by David Mostyn

Ladybird Books

Counting in 2s, 3s and 5s

Count in **2s** from the START sign and put a **red circle** round each number you land on. ◯

Now count in **3s**. Put a **blue square** round each number you land on. ☐

Finally, count in **5s**. Put a **yellow triangle** round each number you land on. △

Which numbers have a ◯, a ☐ and a △ ?

Answer _____

I'VE DONE A FEW FOR YOU!

More counting

Count the number of spots in each group of ladybirds.
Write the number in each speech bubble.

4   8   12   16

Count the number of buttons in each group.

6   12   18   24

Count the number of petals in each set of flowers.

10   20   30   40   50

Fill in the missing numbers.

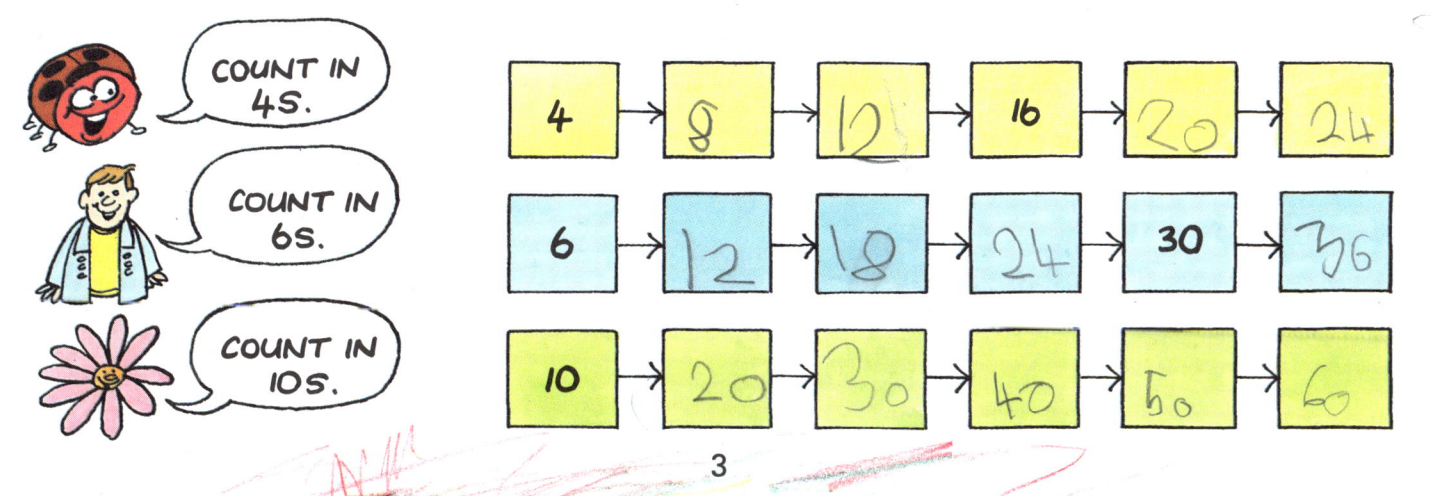

COUNT IN 4S.

| 4 | 8 | 12 | 16 | 20 | 24 |

COUNT IN 6S.

| 6 | 12 | 18 | 24 | 30 | 36 |

COUNT IN 10S.

| 10 | 20 | 30 | 40 | 50 | 60 |

Addition squares

To make an addition square you must add the numbers across the bottom of the square to the numbers up the side.

NUMBER 11 IS PUT IN THE SQUARE 2 SPACES ACROSS THE BOTTOM AND 9 SPACES UP THE SIDE BECAUSE 2+9=11

+	1	2	3	4	5	6	7	8	9	10
10	11	12	13	14	15	16	17	18	19	20
9	10	11	12	13	14	15	16	17	18	19
8	9	10	11	12	13	14	15	16	17	18
7	8	9	10	11	12	13	14	15	16	17
6	7	8	9	10	11	12	13	14	15	16
5	6	7	8	9	10	11	12	13	14	15
4	5	6	7	8	9	10	11	12	13	14
3	4	5	6	7	8	9	10	11	12	13
2	3	4	5	6	7	8	9	10	11	12
1	2	3	4	5	6	7	8	9	10	11

Complete the addition square.

Find these patterns in your square:

▶ 2 4 6 8 10 12 14 16 18 20

▶ 6 6 6 6 6 6 6

▶ 1 3 5 7 9 11 13 15 17 19

▶ 10 10 10 10 10 10 10 10 10 10

ASK AN ADULT TO CHECK YOUR ANSWERS.

SHADE EACH PATTERN WITH A DIFFERENT COLOURED CRAYON.

Now answer these addition sums. Try doing them in your head first, then use your addition square to check your answers.

6 + 5 = 11   6 + 6 = 12   10 + 7 = 17
4 + 5 = 9   8 + 6 = 14   9 + 7 = 16
10 + 5 = 15   4 + 6 = 10   5 + 7 = 12
9 + 5 = 13   9 + 6 = 15   7 + 7 = 14

Which rabbit belongs in which hutch?

Hutches: 5, 8, 12, 15

Rabbits: 3+5, 7+8, 2+6, 4+1, 3+2, 6+6, 9+6, 4+4

You write the questions
Use your addition square to complete these sums.

6 + [4] = 10   ☐ + 4 = 11   10 + ☐ = 12
☐ + 5 = 10   8 + ☐ = 11   ☐ + 9 = 12
3 + ☐ = 10   ☐ + 2 = 11   4 + ☐ = 12
☐ + 8 = 10   5 + ☐ = 11   ☐ + 2 = 12

Co-ordinates

Here is a map of an island.
The beach hut is in square (4,2).
That is **4** squares **across** and **2** squares **up**.

THE NUMBERS ACROSS AND UP ARE CALLED CO-ORDINATES.

THE FIRST NUMBER TELLS YOU HOW MANY ACROSS, THE SECOND NUMBER TELLS YOU HOW MANY UP.

REMEMBER, ACROSS FIRST, THEN UP.

Find these places on the map and write their co-ordinates.

swimming pool __(2,3)__   Mount High Peak _____   shipwreck _____

Shark Bay _____   campsite _____   lighthouse _____

ice cream bar _____   bridge _____   cave _____

Co-ordinate codes

You can use co-ordinates to write messages in secret code.

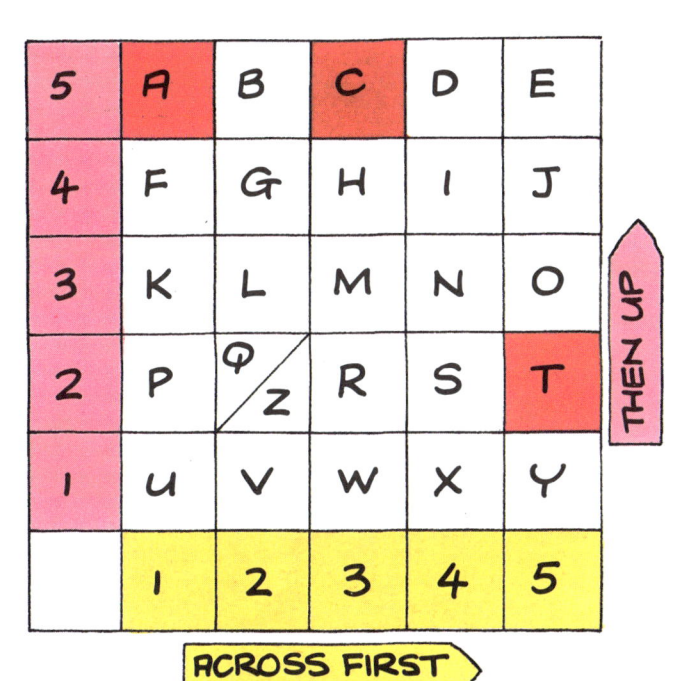

C is in square (3,5)

A is in square (1,5)

T is in square (5,2)

So "CAT" written in code is: (3,5) (1,5) (5,2)

Work out what this message says.

(3,1) (3,4) (1,5) (5,2) / (4,4) (4,2) / (5,2) (3,4) (5,5) /
___ ___ ___ ___   ___ ___   ___ ___ ___

(2,5) (5,5) (4,2) (5,2) / (5,1) (5,5) (1,5) (3,2) /
___ ___ ___ ___   ___ ___ ___ ___

(1,4) (5,3) (3,2) / (1,3) (1,5) (4,3) (2,4) (1,5) (3,2) (5,3) (5,3) (4,2)
___ ___ ___   ___ ___ ___ ___ ___ ___ ___ ___ ___ ?

(1,5) / (2,3) (5,5) (1,5) (1,2) / (5,1) (5,5) (1,5) (3,2)
___   ___ ___ ___ ___   ___ ___ ___ ___ !

Write this message in code.
  M   A   T   H   S   I   S   F   U   N
( ) ( ) ( ) ( ) ( ) / ( ) ( ) / ( ) ( ) ( )

Sorting shapes

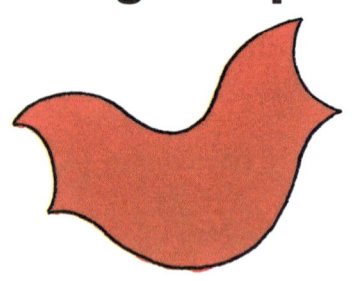

THIS SHAPE HAS CURVED SIDES.

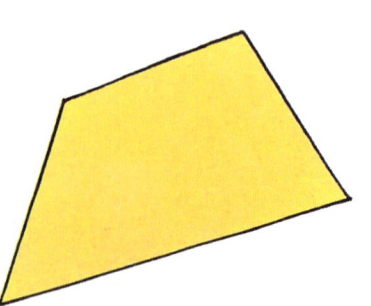

THIS SHAPE HAS STRAIGHT SIDES.

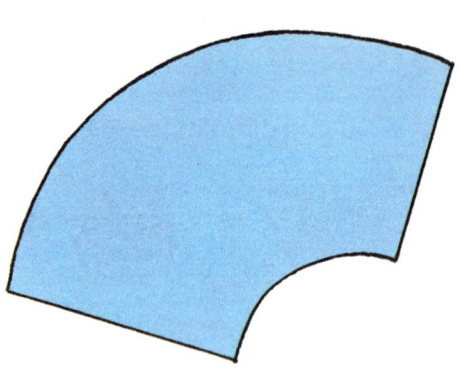

THIS SHAPE HAS CURVED AND STRAIGHT SIDES.

Look carefully at these shapes.

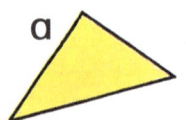

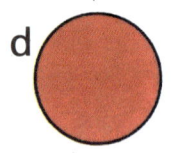

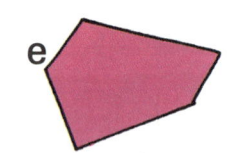

a   b   c   d   e   f   g

Which shapes have . . .

curved sides only?_____

straight sides only?_____

curved and straight sides?_____

DRAW SOME SHAPES OF YOUR OWN ON A BLANK SHEET OF PAPER.

Dotty doodles

Can you make these shapes into something else?

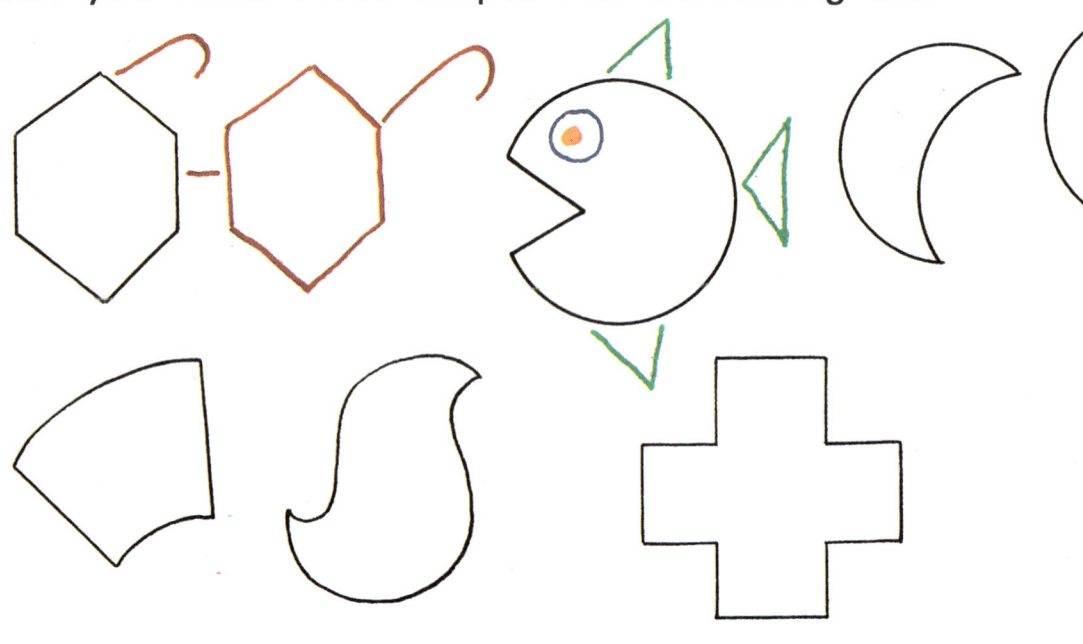

I'VE DONE SOME FOR YOU.

Look at these shapes.

triangles

circles

rectangles

COUNT THE SIDES. HOW MANY SIDES DOES A TRIANGLE HAVE?

THREE!

squares

pentagons

hexagons

CIRCLES ARE TRICKY. THEY HAVE ONE CURVED SIDE.

How many of each shape can you find in the picture below?

triangles ☐   squares ☐   rectangles ☐
circles ☐   pentagons ☐   hexagons ☐

9

Hundreds, tens and units

Look at this number.

THIS TELLS YOU HOW MANY UNITS.

THIS TELLS YOU HOW MANY HUNDREDS.

THIS TELLS YOU HOW MANY TENS.

How many hundreds in these numbers?

376 ☐ hundreds   750 ☐ hundreds   912 ☐ hundreds

495 ☐ hundreds   824 ☐ hundreds   124 ☐ hundreds

Now put all the numbers in order, starting with the smallest.

☐ → ☐ → ☐ → ☐ → ☐ → ☐

SMALLEST

LOOK AT THE HUNDREDS.

How many tens in these numbers?

167 ☐ tens   105 ☐ tens   131 ☐ tens

129 ☐ tens   144 ☐ tens   192 ☐ tens

Now put all the numbers in order, starting with the biggest.

☐ → ☐ → ☐ → ☐ → ☐ → ☐

BIGGEST

LOOK AT THE TENS.

How many units in these numbers?

765 ☐ units   769 ☐ units   763 ☐ units

762 ☐ units   760 ☐ units   766 ☐ units

Now put all the numbers in order, starting with the smallest.

☐ → ☐ → ☐ → ☐ → ☐ → ☐

SMALLEST

LOOK AT THE UNITS.

Order! Order!

Bill   Jan   Sue   Tariq   Kylie   Jason   Phil   Ann   Tom   Jez

Bill is holding the card for 0. Jez is holding the card for 1000. Kylie is roughly in the middle, holding the card for 500.

How many children are there? ☐

How many children are not holding cards? ☐

Here are some more cards:

750   400   650   350   990

Put the cards in order, starting with the smallest number.

☐ → ☐ → ☐ → ☐ → ☐
SMALLEST

Who should hold the first of these cards so that it will be roughly in the correct place?

_____

Who should hold the other cards so that they will be roughly in the correct place?

_____ should hold the second card.

_____ should hold the third card.

_____ should hold the fourth card.

_____ should hold the fifth card.

11

grannie Ailsa
Taking away

TAKE AWAY SUBTRACT MINUS DIFFERENCE

These are all words we can use when we need to take one number away from another.

$\begin{array}{r}15\\-3\\\hline 12\end{array}$

15 **take away** 3 equals 12
subtract 3 from 15 equals 12
15 **minus** 3 equals 12
(15,3) **difference** 12

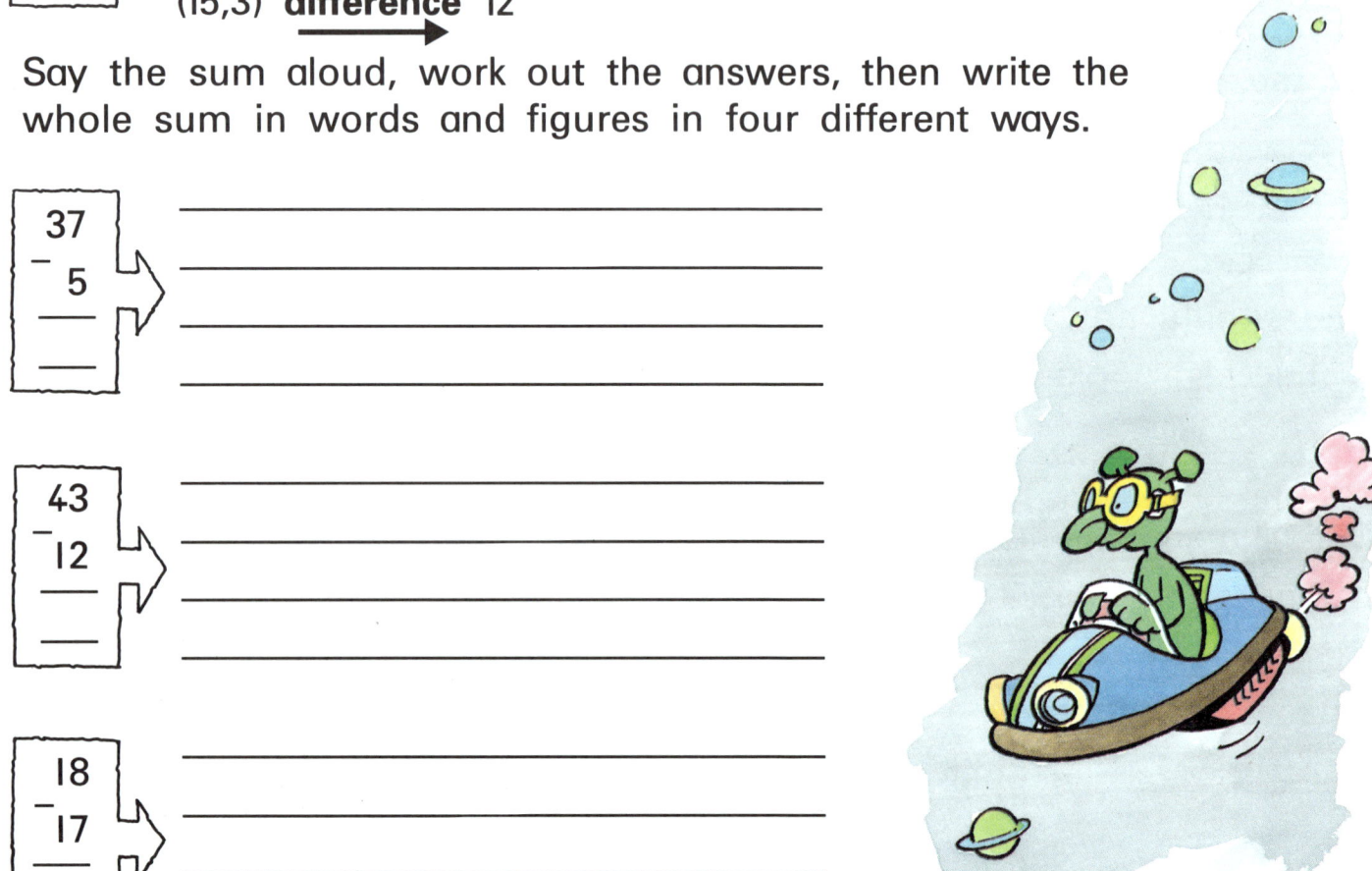

Say the sum aloud, work out the answers, then write the whole sum in words and figures in four different ways.

$\begin{array}{r}37\\-5\\\hline\end{array}$

$\begin{array}{r}43\\-12\\\hline\end{array}$

$\begin{array}{r}18\\-17\\\hline\end{array}$

Now try these.

T U	T U	T U	T U	T U
2 7	3 2	2 0	1 5	1 9
−1 6	−2 0	−1 0	− 5	−1 2

T U	T U	T U	T U
6 3	9 0	5 7	7 1
−1 2	−7 0	−3 1	−1 0

REMEMBER, ALWAYS BEGIN WITH THE UNITS.

SAY THE SUMS ALOUD AS MANY DIFFERENT WAYS AS YOU CAN.

Read the stories below, answer the questions, then draw a line to the sum above that tells the story in numbers.

The queen baked nineteen jam tarts.
The knave stole twelve.
How many were left? ☐

The squirrels found twenty seven nuts.
One greedy squirrel ate sixteen.
How many were left? ☐

Measuring round the corner

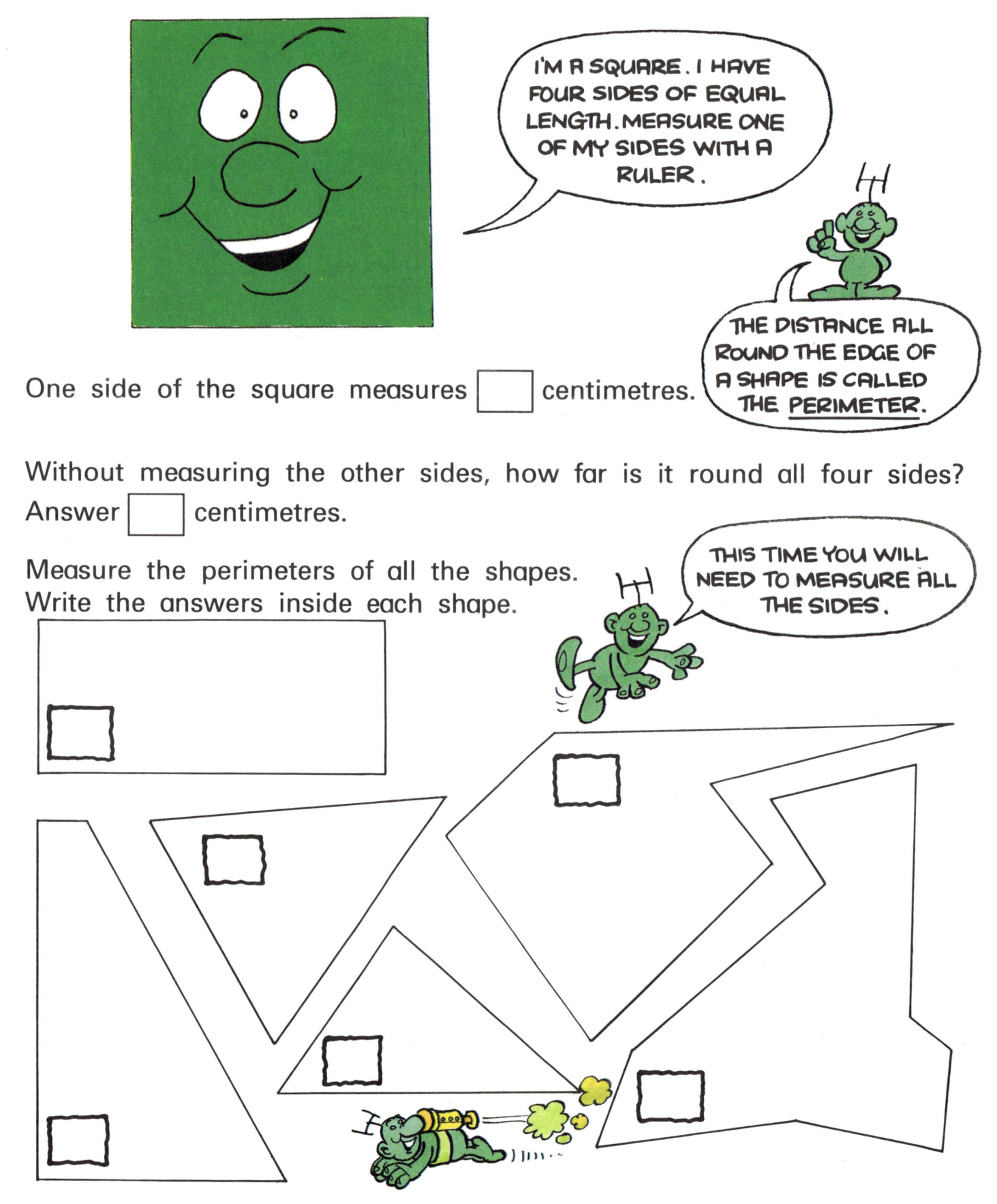

I'M A SQUARE. I HAVE FOUR SIDES OF EQUAL LENGTH. MEASURE ONE OF MY SIDES WITH A RULER.

THE DISTANCE ALL ROUND THE EDGE OF A SHAPE IS CALLED THE PERIMETER.

One side of the square measures ☐ centimetres.

Without measuring the other sides, how far is it round all four sides?
Answer ☐ centimetres.

Measure the perimeters of all the shapes.
Write the answers inside each shape.

THIS TIME YOU WILL NEED TO MEASURE ALL THE SIDES.

Colour the shape with the longest perimeter red.

14

Wanted!

Fill in this wanted sign.
Make up the name but measure and describe somebody real.

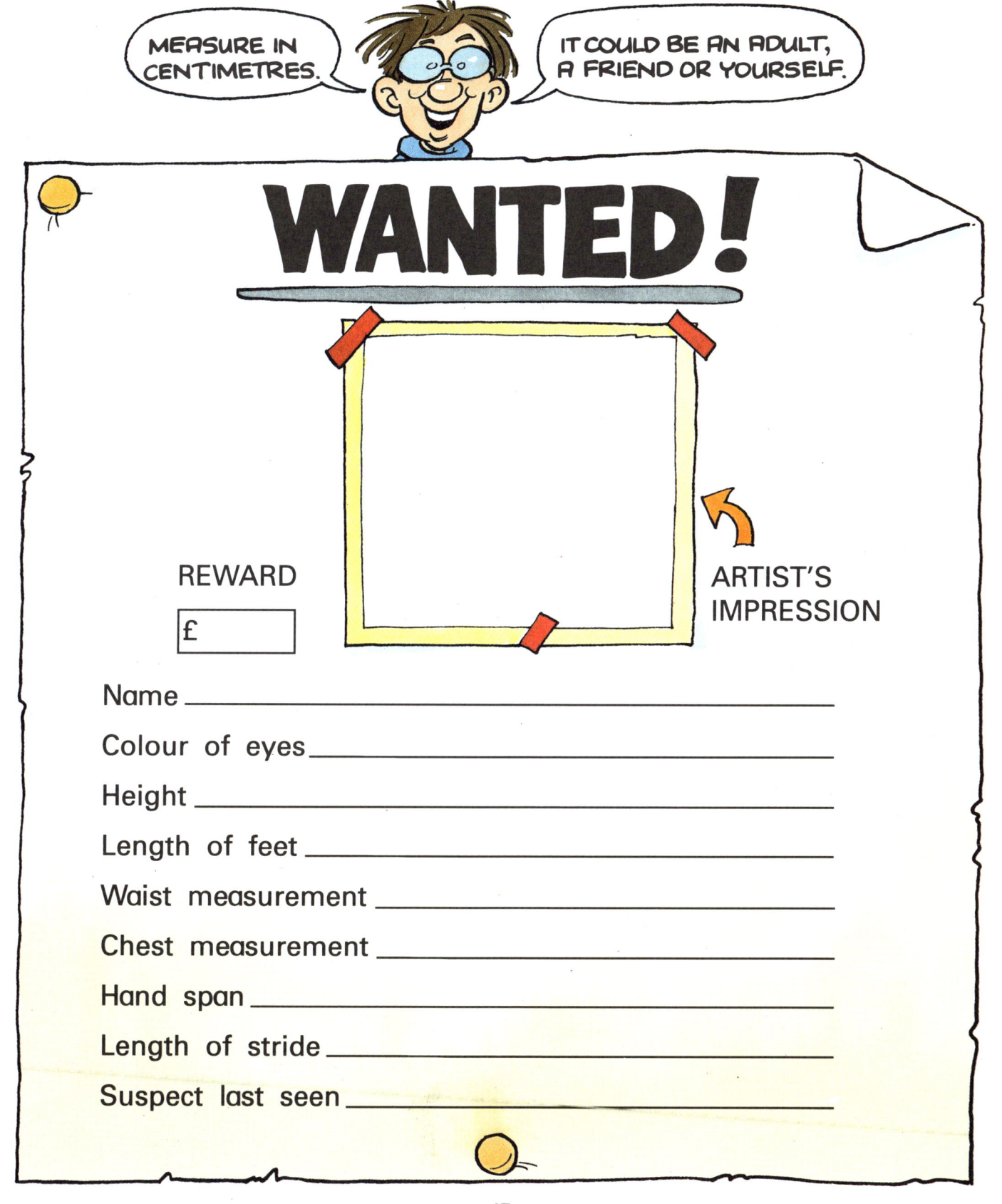

MEASURE IN CENTIMETRES.

IT COULD BE AN ADULT, A FRIEND OR YOURSELF.

WANTED!

REWARD

£ _____

ARTIST'S IMPRESSION

Name _____

Colour of eyes _____

Height _____

Length of feet _____

Waist measurement _____

Chest measurement _____

Hand span _____

Length of stride _____

Suspect last seen _____

Multiplication tables

Here are the tables from 2 to 12. Fill in the answers, then ask an adult to check them. You can use these pages to learn your tables by heart.

ASK A FRIEND TO TEST YOU.

0 × 2 =	0 × 3 =	
1 × 2 =	1 × 3 =	
2 × 2 =	2 × 3 =	
3 × 2 =	3 × 3 =	
4 × 2 =	4 × 3 =	
5 × 2 =	5 × 3 =	
6 × 2 =	6 × 3 =	
7 × 2 =	7 × 3 =	
8 × 2 =	8 × 3 =	
9 × 2 =	9 × 3 =	
10 × 2 =	10 × 3 =	
11 × 2 =	11 × 3 =	
12 × 2 =	12 × 3 =	

33?

0 × 4 =	0 × 5 =	0 × 6 =
1 × 4 =	1 × 5 =	1 × 6 =
2 × 4 =	2 × 5 =	2 × 6 =
3 × 4 =	3 × 5 =	3 × 6 =
4 × 4 =	4 × 5 =	4 × 6 =
5 × 4 =	5 × 5 =	5 × 6 =
6 × 4 =	6 × 5 =	6 × 6 =
7 × 4 =	7 × 5 =	7 × 6 =
8 × 4 =	8 × 5 =	8 × 6 =
9 × 4 =	9 × 5 =	9 × 6 =
10 × 4 =	10 × 5 =	10 × 6 =
11 × 4 =	11 × 5 =	11 × 6 =
12 × 4 =	12 × 5 =	12 × 6 =

54?

0 × 7 = ☐	0 × 8 = ☐	0 × 9 = ☐
1 × 7 = ☐	1 × 8 = ☐	1 × 9 = ☐
2 × 7 = ☐	2 × 8 = ☐	2 × 9 = ☐
3 × 7 = ☐	3 × 8 = ☐	3 × 9 = ☐
4 × 7 = ☐	4 × 8 = ☐	4 × 9 = ☐
5 × 7 = ☐	5 × 8 = ☐	5 × 9 = ☐
6 × 7 = ☐	6 × 8 = ☐	6 × 9 = ☐
7 × 7 = ☐	7 × 8 = ☐	7 × 9 = ☐
8 × 7 = ☐	8 × 8 = ☐	8 × 9 = ☐
9 × 7 = ☐	9 × 8 = ☐	9 × 9 = ☐
10 × 7 = ☐	10 × 8 = ☐	10 × 9 = ☐
11 × 7 = ☐	11 × 8 = ☐	11 × 9 = ☐
12 × 7 = ☐	12 × 8 = ☐	12 × 9 = ☐

THAT'S MY AGE.

0 × 10 = ☐	0 × 11 = ☐	0 × 12 = ☐
1 × 10 = ☐	1 × 11 = ☐	1 × 12 = ☐
2 × 10 = ☐	2 × 11 = ☐	2 × 12 = ☐
3 × 10 = ☐	3 × 11 = ☐	3 × 12 = ☐
4 × 10 = ☐	4 × 11 = ☐	4 × 12 = ☐
5 × 10 = ☐	5 × 11 = ☐	5 × 12 = ☐
6 × 10 = ☐	6 × 11 = ☐	6 × 12 = ☐
7 × 10 = ☐	7 × 11 = ☐	7 × 12 = ☐
8 × 10 = ☐	8 × 11 = ☐	8 × 12 = ☐
9 × 10 = ☐	9 × 11 = ☐	9 × 12 = ☐
10 × 10 = ☐	10 × 11 = ☐	10 × 12 = ☐
11 × 10 = ☐	11 × 11 = ☐	11 × 12 = ☐
12 × 10 = ☐	12 × 11 = ☐	12 × 12 = ☐

GULP!

Division

Here are eight hats. If they were shared equally among four friends, how many hats would each friend have?

÷ IS THE SIGN FOR SHARING OR DIVIDING.

Each friend would have two hats.

This can be written as a sum:
8 hats shared among 4 friends = 2 hats → **8 ÷ 4 = 2**

Share these straws equally among seven glasses.
How many straws in each glass?
14 ÷ 7 = ☐

Share these pieces of cheese equally among five mice.
How many pieces will each mouse get?
15 ÷ 5 = ☐

Divide these flags equally among six boats.
How many flags on each boat?
12 ÷ 6 = ☐

Divide these bees equally among three flowers.
How many bees on each flower?
30 ÷ 3 = ☐

Colour by numbers

Complete the sums to find out which colours to use.

Example: 18 ÷ 6 = 3 = red

number	1	2	3	4	5	6	7
colour	orange	yellow	red	green	brown	blue	black

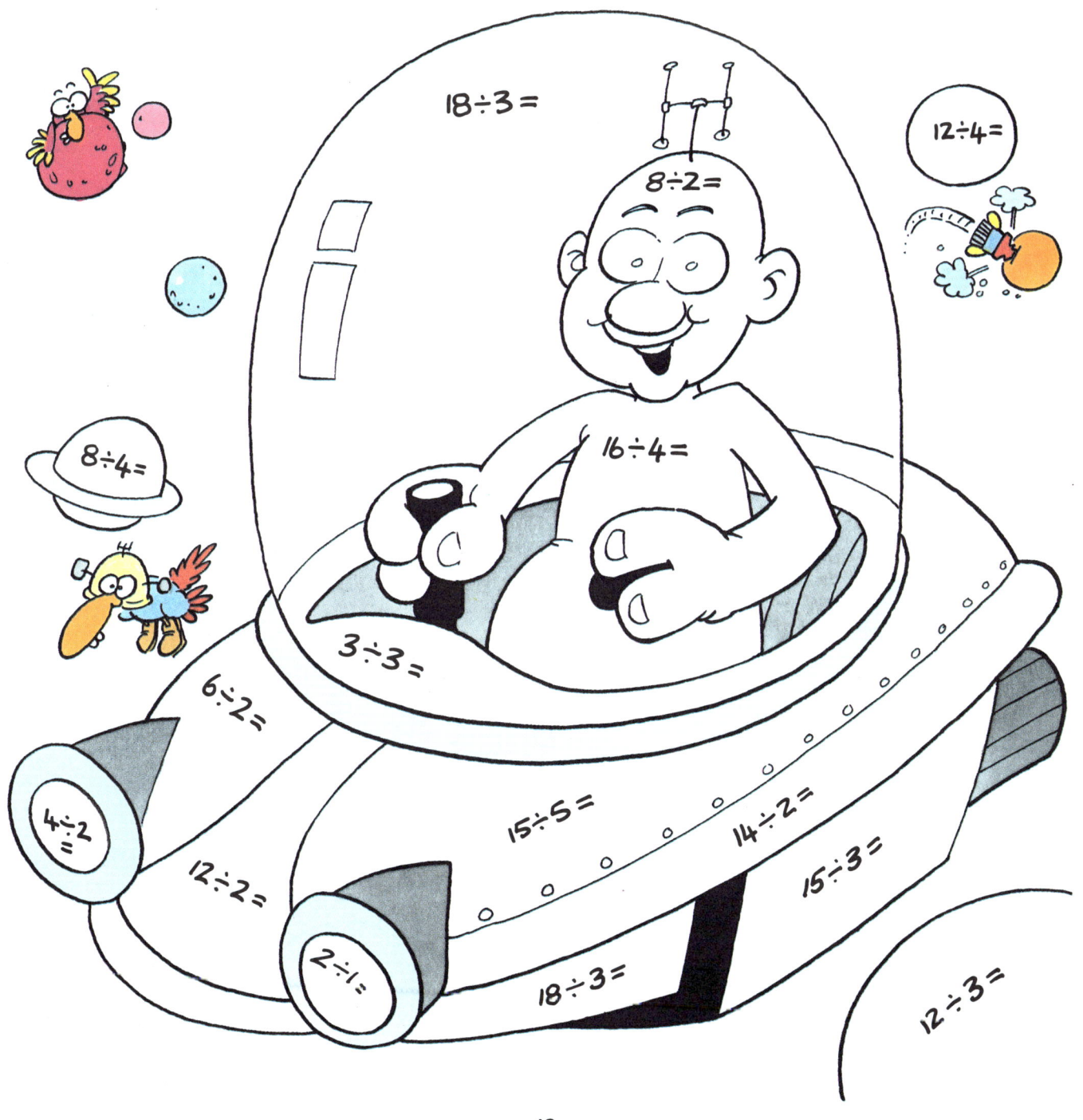

18 ÷ 3 =

12 ÷ 4 =

8 ÷ 2 =

16 ÷ 4 =

8 ÷ 4 =

3 ÷ 3 =

6 ÷ 2 =

4 ÷ 2 =

15 ÷ 5 =

14 ÷ 2 =

15 ÷ 3 =

12 ÷ 2 =

2 ÷ 1 =

18 ÷ 3 =

12 ÷ 3 =

Fractions

This apple has been cut into **2 equal parts**.
Each part is called a **half**.
The sign for half is ½.

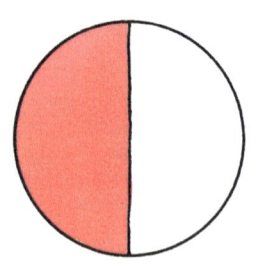

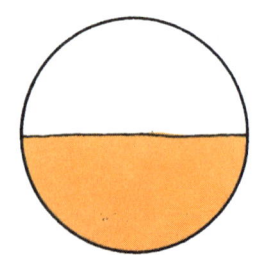

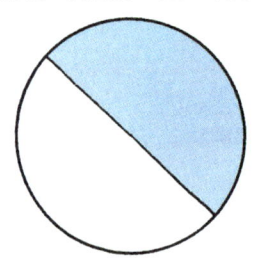

Half of each circle is coloured and half is white.

1 → 1 whole
– → divided into
2 → 2 equal parts

Colour one half of each of these shapes.

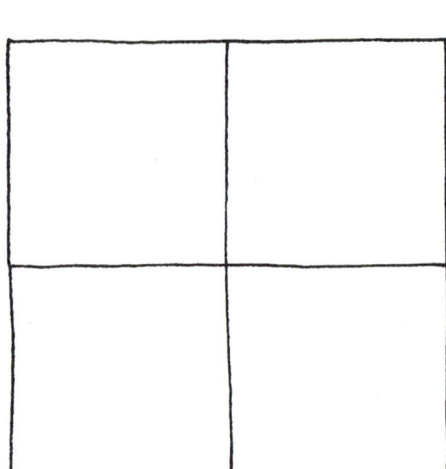

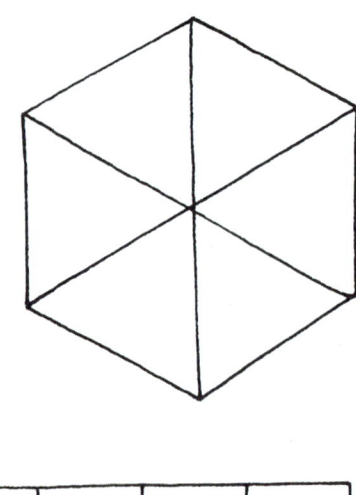

This cake is cut into **4 equal parts**.
Each part is called a **quarter**.
The sign for a quarter is ¼.

1 → 1 whole
– → divided into
4 → 4 equal parts

A quarter of each circle is coloured.
The three quarters left are white.

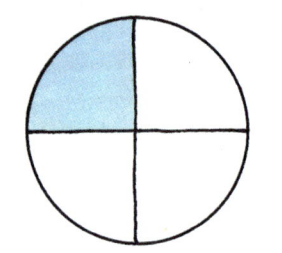

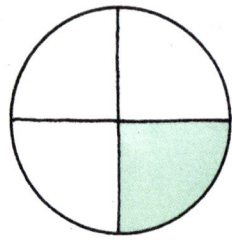

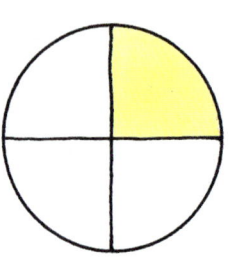

WE CAN WRITE THREE QUARTERS LIKE THIS: ¾

Colour one quarter of each of these shapes.

What fraction of these shapes is coloured?

Making patterns

Colour one half of each big square.
Make a different pattern each time.

I'VE DONE TWO FOR YOU.

COUNT ALL THE SMALL SQUARES FIRST. FIND HALF OF THAT NUMBER.

Measuring weight

You will need:

kitchen scales   marbles   crayons   cotton reels   cornflakes

Look at the weighing scales and find the 50g mark.
First **estimate** how many of each object you will need to make 50g.
Write down all your estimates. Then weigh out 50g of each item.

ESTIMATE MEANS GUESS.

Object	Estimate	How many makes 50g?
marbles		
crayons		
cotton reels		
cornflakes		

Put a ring round the things that you think weigh more than 100g.

Which do you think weighs the most? _____

Odd or even?

Find the hidden picture by colouring all the **even** numbered shapes **red** and the **odd** numbered shapes **blue**.

Graphs

Kate asked some friends which were their favourite animals. The graph shows what she found out.

THIS IS CALLED A BLOCK GRAPH.

VOTE FOR ME!

1 Which animals were the most popular? _____

2 Which animals were the least popular? _____

3 How many people liked dogs best? ☐

4 How many people liked cats best? ☐

5 The same number of people chose two animals.

   Which animals were they? _____

6 How many people took part in Kate's survey? ☐